ALMOST DEAD

The Final Conversation Before the Author's Planned Death

ALMOST DEAD

The Final Conversation Before the Author's Planned Death

Cary Harrison

in dialogue with

Derek Scott

Imprint: Ivy Signal Editions ISBN: 979-8-9955794-1-0

For Derek's Daughter, Maya.

For my listeners.

And for anyone who must learn to let go before they are ready.

Table of Contents

Prologue

The Parking Lot

Radio trains you to be comfortable inside discomfort. You learn early that silence is not your enemy, that grief makes for better listening than triumph, that the human voice at its most unguarded is the most powerful instrument you will ever point a microphone at. After thirty-plus years behind the mic—network news, satellite, commercial radio, AM Talk, current long, beautiful indiscipline of KPFK Los Angeles Public radio—I thought I had heard most of what a person could say. I thought I had sat across from enough pain to know its particular grammar. I was wrong.

A year and a half ago, on one of the custom tours I design for HE Travel—the kind where I take people to discover places they might not find on their own, where the itinerary is a door, and the real journey is whatever happens, once you walk through it—I met a man who became my fast favorite. His name was Derek Scott. He was a psychotherapist from Canada, a man of middle years and considerable interior architecture, and from the first morning he was simply good company. Effortlessly funny. Not loud, not needy, not performing. Just sharp and warm and reliably, quietly, quick on the uptake.

Derek Scott (Czech Republic)

For thirteen days across Central Europe—Prague, Vienna, the old quarter of Budapest, a monastery outside Brno that hadn't changed its lunch menu in six hundred years—he was simply part of the group. He laughed at dinner. He lingered in museums longer than anyone else, standing in front of things most tourists photograph and move on from, actually looking. He drank beer in old squares that had watched empires assemble and dissolve. He kept up. He carried his own bag. He never once asked for accommodation, never flagged, never retreated.

There was no visible fragility. No signal buried in the jokes, no careful management of distance. Whatever he was carrying, he carried it invisibly, and he carried it without burdening a single person in that group. That is not a small thing. Most of us, under the weight he was under, would have leaked. We would have said something, found some way to let the pressure off. He said nothing. He simply showed up, every day, at full capacity, and made thirteen strangers feel like they had known him for years.

On the final afternoon, just before our farewell dinner, he pulled me aside in the hotel parking lot. The light was going flat, the way it does in Central Europe at the end of summer, amber going gray, the air still warm but the sky already thinking about autumn. He said this would be a real farewell. I asked him what that meant. He said he would be dead within three months. Then he gave me the date. Then he gave me the time.

Because he had a great sense of humor—and because I'm used to being set up—I waited for the punchline. There wasn't one. It was delivered flat. Calm. Inventory, not drama. He was not confessing. He was not unburdening. He was simply choosing to tell me, before the trip formally ended, so that we could have an honest goodbye. So I wouldn't be caught off guard by the news later, scrolling through email on some ordinary Tuesday.

I don't cry easily as an adult. I just don't. But I felt my throat close in a way I recognized: grief arriving before comprehension, the body understanding before the mind catches up. This was a man I genuinely liked. And he had just informed me that the clock was not theoretical. He had stage four cancer. He had taken this trip as his last voyage. And for thirteen days, he never once revealed the magnitude of what he was living with. No confession. No spotlight. No martyrdom. He simply traveled and let the rest of us do the same.

What you are about to read is the record of a conversation we had three and a half weeks before his scheduled death. It is not a political argument. It is not a moral provocation. It is not a position paper dressed in the borrowed clothes of memoir. It is the record of the choices he made to organize his own dying—the time, the circumstances, the people in the room, the blue fluid, the eight minutes—and, more importantly, the reasoning behind those choices. There is no template for this kind of conversation. We discovered that together, in real time, with a webcam between us and the clock running. This is where it begins.

Introduction

The Sentence

The room didn't feel sacred. There was no candlelight, no hushed reverence, no orchestral underscore waiting for the cue. There was a webcam, a desk, a compliment about a blazer, and a quick run for coffee. The technician in me was watching frame rates. The journalist in me was thinking about structure. And then Derek Scott said something that stopped both of them cold.

> *"I thought we could open with something really powerful like—I'm going to be dead in three and a half weeks."*

It was offered almost casually. A dry suggestion for an opening line. A writer's instinct. A little mischief in the delivery, the trace of a smile, the kind of understatement that only works when the speaker is fully in command of what they're understating. But it wasn't rehearsal. It wasn't theater. It was inventory.

Interview: Cary Harrison/Derek Scott

Three and a half weeks. Not metaphor. Not prognosis measured in the blurry arithmetic of months. Not the vague terminality that medicine sometimes offers as a kindness, the way oncologists speak in ranges—six months to a year, possibly more, it's hard to say. Derek had an appointment. He had a date on a calendar the way you have a dental cleaning or a flight to catch. And he had chosen to open our conversation with it the same way a good editor opens a story: with the most important fact, stated plainly, without evasion.

Most people live inside indefinite time. Even after a serious diagnosis, even after the word terminal has been spoken aloud in a clinical room, there is still an elastic quality to the horizon. A window. A probability. A hope. The human nervous system is extraordinarily good at converting finitude into something it can manage at a distance. We know we are mortal in the same abstract way we know that geological time is real: intellectually, thoroughly, and without any visceral connection to what that actually means on a Tuesday afternoon.

Derek did not have probability. He had scheduling. He had negotiated with his physician, with the legal architecture of the Canadian medical system, with his own psychology, and with his family, to arrive at a specific date and a specific time. And he had decided—with the deliberateness that characterized everything else I had observed about him—that the best thing he could do with the weeks remaining was to talk about it honestly, on the record, so that something useful might survive him.

I said something that surprised me with its transparency: "I haven't done this kind of interview before... there's no template." That admission, which I did not plan, is in some sense the moral center of this book. There is no template. Not culturally, not medically, not psychologically. We know how to celebrate birth. We know how to celebrate achievement, romance, resilience, recovery. We have ceremonies for almost everything. We do not know how to speak calmly, openly, and without flinching about deliberate dying—about choosing the terms of your own exit. And yet here it was, offered to me with the same ease Derek brought to everything: just the truth, presented without theater, and a request that we try to do it justice.

CHAPTER ONE: Knowing the Date

To know you are dying is one category of experience. To know when you are dying is another entirely. These are not the same thing, and the distance between them is not measured in time. It is measured in the quality of attention you are able to bring to what remains.

Derek's diagnosis was not ambiguous. "I have two forms of cancer," he said. "It's metastasized. I have throat cancer with a large tumor—and I have lung cancer." The throat tumor was the immediate threat: it had grown into the proximity of a major artery, and his physicians had been clear about what that meant for the probable shape of his death. Without intervention, the end would most likely arrive one of two ways. A stroke that would erase the person his family knew—the voice, the wit, the precision of his thinking—while leaving behind a body in a bed. Or an arterial rupture that would empty him onto the floor before anyone could intervene.

"I do not want to die that way. I don't want my child to find me on the floor... bleeding out."

This is the moment where ethical debates typically ignite. The right to die, the sanctity of life, the role of physicians in hastening death, the moral hazard of a system that permits it. Those debates are real and they are not without substance. But in the room—in the actual room, between two human beings, one of whom was speaking from three and a half weeks out—there was no debate. There was a father. There was foreseeable trauma. There was a choice about whether that trauma would be imposed on the people he loved or whether he could structure his exit to spare them.

Derek lived in Canada, where Medical Assistance in Dying—MAID—is enshrined in law and surrounded by structured safeguards. Two independent physicians must assess and confirm the terminal diagnosis. The patient must demonstrate that consent is voluntary, informed, and not coerced. Mental competence must be intact at the time of the request and again at the time of the procedure. There are waiting periods. There is documentation. There is, in other words, a system designed not to make death easy but to make chosen death possible, for those whose alternatives have narrowed to forms of suffering they find intolerable.

What the system provides, beyond the procedure itself, is something more surprising: it provides time. When you know the date, you are released from the particular agony of waiting for something that might happen at any moment. You are freed from the hypervigilance of terminal uncertainty—the way every headache becomes a possible harbinger, every morning a small negotiation. Derek knew when. And knowing when meant he could decide how to spend the time before then. He could have a conversation like this one. He could take a tour of Central Europe. He could say goodbye to the people he wanted to say goodbye to, with the full use of his faculties and his voice.

Intention is what unsettles people most about this arrangement. Randomness feels natural. It feels like something that happened to you, which absolves everyone of responsibility. Choice feels transgressive—it feels like agency where we have collectively decided agency should not exist. But Derek's choice was not transgressive. It was, if anything, an act of extraordinary consideration: the decision not to impose the worst of his dying on the people who would have to watch it.

CHAPTER TWO:
The Procedure

When people hear the phrase "medical assistance in dying," imagination fills in the blanks with whatever their particular dread contains. They picture drama, chaos, moral collapse, a clinical horror show. They picture something that looks like a scene from a bad film about the future. Derek offers something far less cinematic, and far more human.

Health Canada (Wikipedia)

"You have to book the appointment... and that feels surreal."

Booking. Calendar. Time slot. The vocabulary of administrative life—the same language you use to schedule a haircut or a car service appointment—applied to the last day of your existence. It is jarring, and Derek knows it is jarring, and he says it with exactly the right amount of dryness to let you sit with the absurdity without flinching from it. The surrealism is the point. Our systems are not built for this. The calendar app does not have a category for it. And yet there it is, on the schedule, like anything else.

He describes the day with the calm specificity of someone who has thought through every detail and made peace with each one. At 2:30, the nurses arrive and place IV ports in both arms—the small plastic fittings that will receive the syringes. There is no urgency to this. It is clinical and careful and, by his account, entirely gentle. Family is present. The room has been arranged to feel as little like a medical setting as possible.

At 3:00, the physician arrives. Derek calls her "Dr. Death" with the kind of affection that only works between people who have established real trust, and the nickname lands as a term of endearment rather than a provocation. She administers the first medication: something that puts him to sleep. Then the second: the one that stops his heart. He describes it simply—"the blue fluid"—without drama, without the lexical armor that medical language usually provides. Blue fluid. That will stop my heart. The precision is almost gentle.

> *"The whole process takes eight minutes."*

Eight minutes. Hold that against the modern Western death, which typically unfolds across weeks and sometimes months of escalating intervention: ICU alarms cycling through the night, intubation, the sedation that removes consciousness but not the body's distress, the confusion of someone who no longer recognizes the faces around them, the restrained limbs, the ventilator rhythms, the fluorescent corridor outside the door where family members receive whispered updates in a register halfway between hope and apology.

Eight minutes is not speed as convenience. It is containment of suffering as a form of grace. It is the decision to let the process of dying be proportionate to the life that preceded it—structured, witnessed, and over before it can become something no one present will be able to forget. The procedure is not about ending life prematurely. It is about ending it before biology becomes violent. And that distinction, which is easy to say and harder to fully receive, is the pivot on which this entire conversation turns.

CHAPTER THREE: The Battle: What We Were Taught to Fight

Language shapes experience more than we are willing to admit. The words we use to describe illness, death, and survival are not neutral containers. They carry ideology inside them, quietly, the way furniture carries the aesthetic assumptions of the decade it was built in. We live inside our metaphors without noticing we have moved in.

Derek returns repeatedly to one phrase that he finds not merely inaccurate but actively damaging. It appears in obituaries, in fundraising campaigns, in the language of oncology waiting rooms, in the captions under photographs of people wearing bandanas and smiling bravely for the camera: "She battled hard." "He fought bravely." "She was a warrior." The war metaphor is so deeply embedded in Western medical culture that most people no longer hear it as metaphor at all. It has become the default analogy for cancer, the cognitive furniture of illness.

> *"Does that mean I lost? Does that make me a loser because I didn't win the battle?"*

It is a devastating question because it is so obvious once it is asked. The battle metaphor implies the outcome is moral. That survival is earned. That dying is, at some level, a failure of will—a defeat that a more determined patient could have avoided. This is, of course, biologically absurd. Cancer is not persuaded by bravery. Metastatic disease does not retreat when confronted by optimism. Tumors are not moved by virtue. But the metaphor persists because it is emotionally useful to the people who survive: it gives grief a shape, a cause, an explanation that does not confront the randomness of who gets sick and who does not.

For early-stage patients, the battle framing can be motivating. It provides an identity, a role, a sense that there is something to do besides wait. But for the terminal, it curdles. It becomes, over time, a slow accusation disguised as encouragement. And Derek—who spent his professional life listening to the language people use to describe their inner experience, tracking the gap between what they say and what they mean—was not going to spend his final weeks inside a metaphor he found dishonest.

He is not losing. He is concluding. He is not being defeated by cancer; he is being carried by time toward the end of a life that was, by the evidence of this conversation, exceptionally well-spent. There is a difference between those two things, and the difference is not semantic. It is the difference between dying as failure and dying as completion. Derek chose completion. And he did it without drama, without manifesto, without anything louder than the flat, precise way he uses language: as a tool for telling the truth.

CHAPTER FOUR: The Architecture of Fear

I said what I suspected most listeners were thinking. "You don't present as someone who knows they're going to be dead in three weeks. You're calm. You're cracking jokes. What about some fear?" The question is generous in its assumption: fear must be there, and the absence of its surface evidence implies either performance or pathology. Derek acknowledged neither.

> *"It's not to say I haven't had fear. Certainly have. But it's parts of me that hold the fear."*

This is not metaphor. It is a precise clinical description drawn from Internal Family Systems therapy—a psychological framework developed by Richard Schwartz that understands the human mind not as a single integrated voice but as a community of semi-autonomous parts, each with its own history, its own agenda, and its own emotional register. In IFS, there is a part that fears annihilation. A part that rages at the unfairness of a diagnosis. A part that grieves the unfinished chapters—the daughter's future milestones, the conversations not yet had, the books not yet read. A part that simply wants more time, with the uncomplicated hunger of a child that doesn't want the evening to end.

All of these parts are real. Derek does not deny them. What IFS offers—and what years of practice in both the clinical and the personal application of this framework had given Derek—is a different relationship to those parts. Instead of being the fear, he relates to it. The fear is not at his core, he relates to it. It is in him, recognized and attended to, but it is not him. It is a child inside the system, and like most children, it quiets when it is acknowledged rather than suppressed.

The shift is subtle and it is everything. Most of us, when confronted with existential dread, do one of two things: we collapse into it, letting it occupy the whole of the available space, or we suppress it with such force that it finds structural expression elsewhere—in aggression, in dissociation, in the kind of brittle cheerfulness that everyone around you can see through. Derek has found a third option. He meets the fear. He lets it speak. He does not let it drive.

His steadiness in this conversation is not stoicism and it is not performance and it is not the numbness that sometimes settles over people who have been living with a diagnosis long enough for it to lose its shock value. It is something more specific and harder to acquire: the product of decades of deliberate psychological practice, applied with full force to the most demanding situation those decades could have prepared him for. He is exactly as calm as he appears to be. And the calm is earned.

CHAPTER FIVE: The Year of Subtraction

Death rarely arrives as a single event. For most people with serious illness, it arrives as a process of subtraction—a serial removal of the things that constitute the self, delivered in installments, with intervals between, that allow just enough adaptation to make the next loss newly devastating.

Radiation destroyed Derek's salivary glands. "I haven't eaten anything solid for a year," he says, and then he delivers the punchline with the timing of a working comedian: “I drink Ensure. My choice of supper is pink, white, or brown.” The humor carries grief the way a river carries silt—you don’t see it until it settles. Food is not merely nutrition. Food is culture, it is ritual, it is pleasure, it is the language of hospitality and celebration and comfort. To lose the ability to eat is to lose a dimension of social life that most of us have never had to consciously value because we have never been without it.

Then the voice changed. The tumor pressing on the nerves altered the quality of his speech, the register of his singing. “I can’t sing like I used to. I love singing.” The loss of song is not trivial. For someone whose professional life was organized around the careful use of language, whose therapeutic practice depended on the quality of his presence and his voice, and who found in music something that language alone cannot quite reach—this is not a minor adjustment. It is the loss of an identity. The person who sang is still present. The singing is not.

Then teaching. He had to give his classes to his senior staff. The work he had spent decades building—the clinical training, the frameworks, the accumulated institutional knowledge of how to help people understand their own minds—was redistributed to others, not because he was ready to let go of it but because the body had made the decision for him. Each of these losses arrived with what Derek describes as the same emotional sequence: denial and disbelief, then protest, then sadness, then accommodation.

The sequence mirrors classical grief theory—the stages that Kübler-Ross identified in dying patients and that subsequent researchers have found across bereavement of all kinds. But Derek's description is not linear. It does not proceed from shock to acceptance and stop. It is cyclical. Each new loss—the food, the voice, the work, the physical mobility, the future he had planned—resets the pattern. He moves through the stages not once but dozens of times, with each subtraction. Terminal illness is not just dying. It is losing your life in installments while you are still alive to experience the losses.

CHAPTER SIX: Medicine, Mysticism, and Meaning

Derek speaks openly about his use of plant medicines and psychedelic-assisted practices as part of the spiritual and psychological work of his final year. This is not a confession and it is not a provocation. It is the statement of a clinician who has spent years researching altered states in therapeutic contexts, and who, when his own context became terminal, applied the same tools he had recommended to others.

> *"They enable me to return to my gratitude."*

Gratitude, in the face of death, can sound like something bought at an airport bookstore. It can sound like a coping strategy dressed in spiritual language—a way of not looking directly at what is happening. Derek's gratitude does not sound like any of those things. It sounds like something arrived at through genuine reckoning: the gratitude of a person who has looked directly at the thing and found, underneath the fear and the grief and the protest, something that he can honestly be thankful for.

He lists what he is grateful for. His daughter. His dogs. His friends. The ability to serve, which he counts as one of the organizing pleasures of his life. The work he was able to do. The people he was able to help. The trips he was able to take. The beer in the old squares. The conversation we are having right now, recorded and preserved and about to outlast him by whatever measure time applies to recorded voices.

> *"I absolutely know... I'm transitioning to becoming an ancestor."*

He does not claim to understand the mechanics of what comes after. He is not arguing for a specific theological position or inviting debate about the nature of consciousness after death. He claims something more modest and, in its modesty, more convincing: confidence in continuity. The sense that what he has been does not simply stop when his heart does. That he will persist in the people he has shaped, the daughter he has raised, the students he has trained, the clients he has steadied. He will become, as he puts it, an ancestor—something that preceded the living and that the living carry forward without always knowing they are carrying it.

And then, with the intellectual honesty that runs through everything he says: "Why it's time to go now? I don't know. And I can assign that to the mystery." The humility in that sentence is as important as the faith. He is not pretending to understand what he does not understand. He is not retrofitting a narrative of cosmic meaning onto a random biological event. He is holding both things at once: the certainty of continuity and the honest admission that timing is beyond his comprehension. That is a rare and specific kind of wisdom, and it costs something to maintain it.

CHAPTER SEVEN: A Father Leaving

Everything narrows when he speaks about Maya. The clinical vocabulary recedes. The philosophical frameworks pause. The wit that has run underneath almost everything he has said goes quiet, briefly, the way an orchestra drops to let the soloist be heard. And what is left is just a father.

> *"I don't want to say goodbye to my daughter. Really, really don't."*

The repetition is not rhetorical. It is the sound of a man pressing against something he cannot change with the full force of his wanting. Everything else in this conversation has been met with equanimity, met with humor, met with the psychological tools he has spent decades developing and refining. This he meets with just grief. Raw and uncomplicated and entirely sufficient.

He has said something to her that sounds, on first hearing, almost impossibly hard. "Honey... your work is to be able to let me go." He has asked his daughter not to cling, not to make her grief a tether that keeps him from completing his dying cleanly. He has asked this not because he wants to leave—he has made it abundantly clear that he does not want to leave—but because he has sat at enough bedsides, in his years of hospice and clinical work, to know what happens when love refuses to release.

People linger. They stay in states of suffering longer than they need to because the people around them cannot bear the final letting go. Love can become, at the end, a form of detention. The person dying is held in place not by their own desire to remain but by the grief of the people who love them. Derek has watched this happen. He does not want it to happen to Maya, and so he has asked of her the hardest thing a parent can ask of a child: not to hold on.

He knows what the future holds for her, because every child who loses a parent knows it, even if they cannot yet articulate it. "At significant times in her life," he says, and the sentence trails in a way that fills itself in: the graduations, the relationships, the ordinary milestones that acquire a particular gravity when there is an empty chair where a father should have been. He knows she will wish he was there. He knows this with the certainty of a man who has spent his professional life understanding what absence does to people. He is preparing to be an absence. He is doing everything he can to make that absence as workable as possible.

CHAPTER EIGHT: Healthcare and the Geography of Suffering

The conversation widens, as conversations about mortality often do, into the political. Not partisan politics—not the horse-race variety, not the cable-news variety—but the politics of systems, the question of how a society organizes itself around the fact of human suffering and what that organization reveals about what it actually values.

Derek tells me he did some research. He wanted to understand what his illness would have cost if he had lived south of the border. He found a figure for the average cost of cancer treatment in the United States. One hundred and fifty thousand dollars. He says it the way you say something you are still in the process of believing.

"Canada? Free."

The contrast is not delivered as a political attack. Derek is not a polemicist and this is not a polemic. It is something closer to bewilderment. The bewilderment of a man who received, at no direct cost to himself, a year of sophisticated oncological care including radiation, chemotherapy, palliative support, psychological resources, and ultimately the medical assistance for a dying program—and who, looking south, cannot quite comprehend how a country of comparable wealth has arranged things so differently.

> *"What do poor people in your country do?"*

The question is the most devastating thing he says in the entire conversation, and he says it without affect, without accusation, almost gently. What do poor people do when they get cancer in America? Do they spend the money they don't have? Do they skip treatment? Do they work through chemotherapy because the insurance doesn't cover enough but the bills don't stop? Do they die differently than Derek is dying—not by choice, not on a schedule, not with family gathered and a physician named "Dr. Death" who is kind and competent—but on the floor, bleeding out, in exactly the way Derek arranged to avoid?

His argument is not ideological. It is personal, and therefore universal. “You don’t know if you’re going to get cancer,” he says. “It’s advocating for yourself.” Universal healthcare is not charity extended to others. It is insurance you are buying for yourself, against the day that randomness delivers a diagnosis and the system you live inside determines whether that diagnosis becomes a catastrophe or simply a hard time. The geography of your birth should not determine the quality of your dying. Derek knows this with the authority of someone for whom it is not hypothetical.

CHAPTER NINE: Masculinity at the Edge

There is a layer in this conversation that is easy to pass over, because Derek does not call attention to it. But it is worth naming. Derek is a man. A middle-aged Western man, formed by the same cultural expectations that form all middle-aged Western men: the expectation of stoicism, the imperative of competence, the unspoken instruction that suffering is to be managed privately and strength is to be displayed publicly. The man who shows his fear is the man who has failed this basic assessment.

Derek shows his fear. He shows his grief. He speaks openly about losing his voice, losing solid food, losing the ability to teach, losing his future. He tells me, plainly and without the slightest armor, that he does not want to say goodbye to his daughter. There is no performance of toughness in any of it. There is no compensatory display of bravado. There is simply an honest account of what it is like to be a person who is dying, delivered by someone who has decided that the performance of invulnerability serves no one at this point.

In another register, this conversation might be described as brave. But I think Derek would resist that word, for the same reason he resisted the battle metaphor. Bravery implies that the natural state is fear and that something exceptional is required to overcome it. What Derek demonstrates is something different: it is the fruit of having done the interior work, over decades, that makes honesty the path of least resistance. He is not overcoming anything. He is simply not pretending. For a man, in a culture that equates not pretending with weakness, that is an act of significant resistance.

Emotional literacy in the face of extinction is not a common skill. It is taught, practiced, and arrived at through the kind of deliberate cultivation that most people never attempt because most people never believe they will need it. Derek needed it. And the reason this conversation exists, the reason it is worth recording and distributing and reading, is that most of us will also need it—not necessarily in the final weeks of our lives, but in the ordinary crises that make the same demands on the same equipment.

CHAPTER TEN: Ritual and the Human Need for Ceremony

Planned death unsettles modern secular culture because it disrupts randomness. And randomness, we have quietly decided, is the appropriate condition of death—the thing that happens to you, not the thing you arrange. This is a historically unusual position. Across most of human history, in most of the cultures that have left records of how they organized their relationship to mortality, conscious preparation for death was not transgressive. It was expected.

The Japanese samurai class developed elaborate protocols for honorable death. Tibetan Buddhist tradition includes detailed instructions for navigating the dying process and what follows it, practices that require years of prior preparation to execute well. Many Indigenous traditions across North and South America include formal ceremonies for elders preparing to leave the community—ceremonies that honor the transition, mark the threshold, and give the assembled witnesses a role in the passage. The medieval European ars moriendi—the art of dying—was a literary genre, a set of instructions for how to die well, widely distributed and seriously engaged with.

We have lost most of that. We have replaced it with the managed confusion of the modern hospital death: the attempt to stave off the inevitable for as long as possible, followed by a sudden shift to "comfort care" when the attempts have exhausted everyone. There is nothing ceremonial about it. There is no preparation, no gathering, no formal marking of the threshold. There is medicine until the medicine stops working, and then there is a death certificate.

What Derek is doing is modern ritual. He has gathered his family. He has set a time. He has chosen his witnesses. In his hands, the medical setting becomes a ceremonial space. The physician becomes something like an officiant. The IV ports are the threshold technology. And the gathering around him is the community doing what communities have always done at the edge of loss: showing up, being present, and consenting together to let something end.

Ritual does not eliminate grief. It structures it. It gives grief a container, a shared vocabulary, a communal permission to feel what you feel without feeling it alone. The absence of ritual is not the absence of grief—it is grief without structure, spilling into the days and weeks following a death without any of the ceremony that might have helped it metabolize. What Derek is offering his family is not just a cleaner death. It is a grounded grief. And that, in the long run, may be the greater gift.

CHAPTER ELEVEN: The Administrative Surrealism of Dying

Derek mentions estate planning. Insurance timing. Property value considerations. The specific sequence in which certain financial arrangements should be finalized relative to the scheduled date. He mentions it in the same tone he uses for everything else—matter-of-fact, slightly wry, with a compressed awareness of the absurdity.

"You have to book the appointment."

The banality of bureaucracy beside mortality creates a specific kind of surrealism that does not appear in any of the literature on dying. The philosophical texts do not prepare you for the fact that you will be filling out forms. The religious traditions do not mention that the executor needs certain documents in a specific order. The therapeutic frameworks for facing death do not include a module on what to do about the car registration.

And yet this administrative surrealism is, in its own strange way, grounding. Death does not suspend systems. Life has always been bureaucratic at its edges—birth certificates, marriage licenses, the paperwork of property and employment and taxation that constitutes the official record of a life. Death simply adds a final layer. You sign. You file. You finalize. You make sure that the people who will survive you have access to the accounts, the passwords, the documents, the instructions for the things that will need to continue after you no longer can.

There is dignity in this preparedness. Not the grand dignity of philosophical acceptance, but the quieter dignity of practical care—the consideration of a person who does not want the people they love to be left sorting through chaos at the worst possible time. Derek has arranged his administrative life the way he arranged his dying: deliberately, with attention to who will be affected and what they will need. The forms do not understand what they are processing. That is fine. The person filling them does. And that understanding is a final act of service.

CHAPTER TWELVE: Humor as Identity

Derek jokes about renaming radiation treatment rooms after nuclear disasters. He suggests "Chernobyl" as a candidate. He makes a deadpan observation about the narrow flavor range of liquid nutrition. He refers to his physician by a nickname that would be inappropriate in any other context and that, in this context, is an expression of deep affection and dark solidarity.

This is not flippancy. It is not avoidance. It is not the whistling-past-the-graveyard bravado of someone who cannot face what is happening and so has found a lateral route around it. Derek's humor is doing something more specific and more interesting than any of those things. It is asserting continuity. It is the statement, made without words, that the person he has always been is still the person he is now—that the cancer has not colonized his personality, that the diagnosis has not replaced the man.

Humor is one of the few things that cancer cannot take. It can take the salivary glands and the singing voice and the solid food and the teaching and the future. It cannot take the wit, as long as the mind remains. And as long as the wit remains, the identity remains. Every joke Derek makes is proof of life: not life as biological function, but life as the particular, irreducible texture of a specific person in a specific moment, making contact with another specific person through the shared recognition of something absurd.

There is a philosophical tradition, stretching from Socrates through Montaigne to the standup comedians who have made darkness their material, that understands humor and mortality as natural companions. The joke about death is not a denial of death. It is a way of sitting next to it without being consumed by it. It is a way of looking at the thing directly without going blind. Derek has been sitting next to his death for long enough to have developed a working relationship with it. The humor is evidence of that relationship. It is not a mask. It is a mode.

CHAPTER THIRTEEN: The Last Line

As the interview closes, I resist the goodbye. The journalist in me has been trained to find endings—to know when a conversation has arrived at its natural conclusion and to let it land. The human in me is stalling. "I'm going to insist it's not yet," I say, which is the kind of thing you say when you know it is, and you are saying it anyway because the alternative is to say goodbye to someone you know you will never speak to again.

Derek answers with the most perfect line in the conversation. He delivers it without pause, without setup, without the beat that a comedian uses to signal that something funny is coming:

> *"I literally have to go because I have a literal deadline."*

There is something almost architectural in the understatement. The double use of "literal" is not accidental—it is a writer's precision, an insistence on the concrete against the metaphorical, a final small refusal of the kind of soft language that usually surrounds these moments. He is not going to rest. He is not going to be at peace. He is not transitioning or passing or moving on. He has a deadline. The word that journalists use, the word that radio people use, the word that describes the absolute terminal point by which a thing must be done—he has one. It is on the calendar. He is going to meet it.

There is no crescendo. No orchestral swell. No final summation that gathers everything together and resolves it into meaning. Just that line, and then the conversation ends. He has given everything the conversation asked of him: clarity, humor, grief, honesty, psychological precision, clinical knowledge, and the willingness to say difficult things in simple language. And now he has somewhere else to be. The clock—the one he has known about for months, the one he checked into and arranged his life around—is still running.

The microphone goes quiet. The hourglass empties. And what remains is this: the record of a voice that did not flinch.

Afterword
What This Leaves Behind

This book is not a position paper. It is not an argument disguised as sentiment, a policy brief dressed in the borrowed clothes of personal testimony. It is not a campaign for or against anything, though it will inevitably be read as one by people for whom the subject of assisted dying is inseparable from political identity. Those readings are not wrong—the political is embedded in every personal story, especially one that intersects with healthcare law and end-of-life policy. But they are incomplete.

What this is, at its most essential, is a record. A record of a man who faced an ending with unusual clarity—who chose to finish consciously rather than collapse accidentally, who refused the war metaphor, who held his fear instead of being consumed by it, who organized his own departure the way he organized the rest of his life: deliberately, with attention to the people around him, with humor intact and self-deception absent. A man who got on a plane for Central Europe with stage four cancer and gave thirteen strangers thirteen days of excellent company, without once burdening them with the knowledge of what he was carrying.

The voice you heard in these pages is the voice of a psychotherapist who spent his professional life helping other people understand their own minds, and who applied that same unflinching attention to himself when the stakes became as high as they can be. He was not performing equanimity. He had arrived at it through work—years of it, in the practices and frameworks and disciplined interior attention that constitute a life seriously engaged with its own contents.

There is a microphone in the image on the cover of this book. That is not accidental. The microphone is the instrument through which a voice travels beyond the room where it was spoken—beyond the moment, beyond the person, into whatever comes after. Derek spoke into a microphone three and a half weeks before he died. The voice that came through it was, by any measure I have for these things, the voice of someone who had done the work. And the hourglass beside the microphone is equally exact:

time moved, as it always does, without sentiment, and he met it without pretense.

Derek Scott wrote his own account of this journey which was the reason for his unusual request for a pre-posthumous book tour. His account is titled ***Dead (Spoiler Alert): A Psychotherapist's Journey with Cancer.*** In it, he goes deeper than he did in our conversation—into the early diagnosis, the incremental losses, the psychological architecture that steadied him, the anger he had to metabolize, the grief he carried, the gratitude he insisted on returning to. He writes as a clinician, as a father, as a human being who refused euphemism.

If this conversation moved you, or unsettled you, or forced you to confront something you have been postponing thinking about, his book will take you further. You can find it wherever books are sold, or request it through your local bookstore. Derek didn't write his book to provoke. He wrote it to prepare—himself, and perhaps you.

Because whether we schedule it or not, there is an ending. What he offers is not control over death. It is coherence in the face of it. And coherence, as it turns out, may be the rarest gift of all.

— Cary Harrison
Los Angeles, 2026

About the Author

Cary Harrison is a journalist, broadcaster, and satirist with more than three decades in national radio and television.

He is the host of **The Cary Harrison Files** on **Los Angeles Public Radio** & the **Pacifica Radio Network**, where his work blends long-form interviews, cultural criticism, and award-winning satirical commentary.

His career has included **CBS News**, **SiriusXM**, **CNN**, **ABC**, **ESPN**, **NYC**, **KPFK Los Angeles**.

His journalism has earned a **Vanderbilt University Siegenthaler Award,** the **Sigma Delta Chi Award** (Society of Professional Journalists' highest public service honor), **Associated Press 1st Place for Best Commentary,** back-to-back honors from **American Women in Radio & Television,** awards from **the LA Press Club,** recognition from **the United Nations,** and **the Edward R. Murrow Award** for Public Radio excellence. He's listed in "Who's Who in America", is related to Abraham Lincoln on his mother's side and framers of the Constitution on his father's.

He continues to travel, record, and follow conversations wherever they lead.

The conversation, as always, continues.

www.ingramcontent.com/pod-product-compliance
Lightning Source LLC
LaVergne TN
LVHW011052110826
845149LV00015B/3467